CW00498608

Celebrating your year

1956

a very special year for

This book was written by Bernard Bradforsand-Tyler as part of *A Time Traveler's Guide* series of books.

All rights reserved. The author exerts the moral right to be identified as the author of the work.

No parts of this book may be reproduced, stored in any retrieval system, or transmitted in any form or by any means, without prior written permission of Kid Hero Stories Pte. Ltd. Business Registration: 53283983L (Singapore).

This is a work of nonfiction. No names have been changed, no events have been fabricated. The content of this book is provided as a source of information for the reader, however it is not meant as a substitute for direct expert opinion. Although the author has made every effort to ensure that the information in this book is correct at time of printing, and while this publication is designed to provide accurate information in regard to the subject matters covered, the author assumes no responsibility for errors, inaccuracies, omissions, or any other inconsistencies herein and hereby disclaims any liability to any party for any loss, damage, or disruption caused by errors or omissions.

All images contained herein are reproduced with the following permissions:
-   Images included in the public domain.
-   Images obtained under creative commons license.
-   Images included under fair use terms.
-   Images reproduced with owner's permission.
All image attributions and source credits are provided at the back of the book. All images are the property of their respective owners and are protected under international copyright laws.

First printed in 2021 in the USA (ISBN 978-0-6450623-3-5). Self-published through Kindle Direct Publishing and IngramSpark for Kid Hero Stories Pte. Ltd.

Let's flashback to 1956, a very special year.

Was this the year you were born?

Was this the year you were married?

Whatever the reason, this book is a celebration of your year,

THE YEAR 1956.

Turn the pages to discover a book packed with fun-filled fabulous facts. We look at the people, the places, the politics and the pleasures that made 1956 unique and helped shape the world we know today.

So get your time-travel suit on, and enjoy this trip down memory lane, to rediscover what life was like, back in the year 1956.

Canadian Pacific presents Canada's spectacular panorama
from the Scenic Domes of The Canadian

SEE ALL AROUND YOU from high-up Scenic Domes. Air conditioning and glareproof windows keep you cool and comfortable. Views like the one above are numerous along THE

CANADIAN'S 2,881-mile Banff-Lake Louise route...the longest Scenic Dome ride in the world. In daily service between Montreal and Vancouver and Toronto and Vancouver.

A DELUXE DINING ROOM CAR specializing in distinctive Canadian cuisine is available to all passengers on board.

MAIN OBSERVATION LOUNGE is a popular spot aboard THE CANADIAN. Here passengers congregate, to relax and chat.

POPULAR-PRICED MEALS and snacks in the Scenic Dome Skyline Coffee Shop can be enjoyed for less than a dollar.

NEW COACHES have reclining chairs (all seats reserved), full-length leg and foot rests, adjustable head rests. Tourist and first class accommodations also.

For reservations contact your local agent or Canadian Pacific in principal cities in the U. S. or in Canada now.

Route of THE CANADIAN

See all around you from high-up Scenic Domes. Air conditioning and glareproof windows keep you cool and comfortable. Views like the one above are numerous along The Canadian's 2,881-mile Banff-Lake Louise route... the longest Scenic Dome ride in the world. In daily service between Montreal and Vancouver and Toronto and Vancouver.

A deluxe dining room car specializing in distinctive Canadian cuisine is available to all passengers on board. Main observation lounge is a popular spot aboard The Canadian. Here passengers congregate, to relax and chat. Popular-priced meals and snacks in the Scenic Dome Skyline Coffee Shop can be enjoyed for less than a dollar.

New coaches have reclining chairs (all seats reserved), full-length leg and foot rests, adjustable head rests. Tourist and first class accommodations also.

For reservations contact your local agent or Canadian Pacific in principal cities in the U.S. or in Canada now.

Contents

Family Life in 1956 America

Imagine if time-travel was a reality, and one fine morning you wake up to find yourself flashed back in time, back to the year 1956.

What would life be like for a typical family, in a typical town, somewhere in America?

A typical family in 1956.

The mid-century post-war boom delivered us a booming economy, booming birth numbers, booming suburbs, and the booming trappings of the consumerist culture we still live in today.

Our rising middle classes were feeling cashed-up. With an increasing desire to have and to spend, consumer demand continued to reach new highs year after year.

In the year 1956, the population of the US increased by 3 million to 174.7 million people.[1]

Massive suburban developments, built on the outskirts of towns, catered to our increased demand for family homes. Sales were boosted by returned soldiers who had access to low interest loans through the G.I. Bill of 1944.

From 1952-1958, 17,300 homes were built in the massive suburban development of Levittown, Pennsylvania.

Our middle-class dreams were built around everything new and modern. We just loved to show off our latest purchases and gadgets. Production of goods continued to increase, and businesses were profitable. With only 6.2% of the world's population in 1956, the USA was producing almost half the world's goods.

An energetic advertising industry, through TV, radio and print, ensured we always knew what our next purchase could and should be.

[1] worldometers.info/world-population/us-population/.

Joining the television in our families' list of must-haves were: defrost refrigerators, front-loading dryers, fully-automatic washing machines, vacuum cleaners, air-conditioning and heating units, milkshake makers, and a multitude of other kitchen gadgets and home appliances. In addition we needed a family car, motorcycle, bicycles, hiking, camping, picnic gear, and much, much more.

IT'S LIGHTER! IT'S MORE POWERFUL!

The 1956 **EUREKA Super**

New **Cyclonic** Air Action creates
New **double-size** throw-away Dust Bag!
...Rolls easily on four

Still only **$69 95**
MODEL 910

Complete with New Deluxe Tools

Philco Super Marketer

The median income was $4,800 [1] a year, unemployment was 4.2% and falling, with GDP at 2.1%. [2]

Average costs in 1956 [3]	
New house	$11,700
New car	$2,050
Refrigerator	$250
Vacuum cleaner	$80
A gallon of gas	$0.22

But beneath the appearance of domestic bliss, Americans were deeply concerned. The threat of the Soviets was ever present. The Cold War dominated US policies and communist fears gripped the nation throughout the decade and beyond.

By the start of 1956, both the US and USSR had successfully developed and detonated hydrogen bombs. The nuclear arms race was well underway. We would endure another 35 years of tension between the two super-powers before the Cold War finally ended with the dissolution of the Soviet Union in 1991.

[1] census.gov/library/publications.html.
[2] thebalance.com/unemployment-rate-by-year-3305506 and thebalance.com/us-gdp-by-year-3305543.
[3] thepeoplehistory.com and mclib.info/reference/local-history-genealogy/historic-prices/.

HOTPOINT'S EXCLUSIVE NEW SPOT·LESS ACTION OUTMODES ALL OTHER DISHWASHING METHODS!

Skeptical housewives are convinced the new Hotpoint Dishwasher gets *everything* sparkling clean, as no other dishwashing method can!

Hotpoint's new electric dishwasher gets dishes *cleaner*, more *sparkling*, more *sanitary* than dishes washed any other way. Yet you just push a button. Everything's done *for* you—even an *automatic pre-rinse* that does away with hand-rinsing.

Two 5-minute Spot·Less washes—with fresh detergent each time—scrub away every trace of food-soil and film. In water that's hotter than hands can stand, dishes then get two thorough rinses.

Spot·Less second rinse eliminates spots on glass and silver! A few drops of "Rinse-Dry," a super wetting agent, are automatically injected into this rinse. Water spreads so smoothly it can't form drops, can't dry as spots.

Racks roll out separately for easy loading, hold complete service for 8. Many families find they hold a full day's dishes. (Upper rack alone holds 31 glasses.)

Five modern Colortones, Coppertone, white, or satin-chrome finish. 24-inch undercounter models, maple-top mobile models, and 48-inch dishwasher-sinks. See the new Hotpoint Dishwashers soon!

Your eyes tell you! Spotted glass (left) was rinsed in plain water. Sparkling glass (right) was rinsed the new Hotpoint Spot·Less way. It gleams like new!

Every day's a holiday with

Hotpoint

Ranges • Refrigerators • Automatic Washers • Clothes Dryers Customline • Dishwashers • Disposalls® • Water Heaters Food Freezers • Air Conditioners
Hotpoint Co.   Chicago 44
(A Division of General Electric Co.)

Skeptical housewives are convinced the new Hotpoint Dishwasher gets *everything* sparkling clean, as no other dishwashing method can!

Hotpoint's new electric dishwasher gets dishes *cleaner*, more *sparkling*, more *sanitary* than dishes washed any other way. Yet you just push a button. Everything's done *for* you—even an *automatic pre-rinse* that does away with hand-rinsing.

Two 5-minute Spot·Less washes—with fresh detergent each time—scrub away every trace of food-soil and film. In water that's hotter than hands can stand, dishes then get two thorough rinses.

Spot·Less second rinse eliminates spots on glass and silver! A few drops of "Rinse-Dry," a super wetting agent, are automatically injected into this rinse. Water spreads so smoothly it can't form drops, can't dry as spots.

Racks roll out separately for easy loading, hold complete service for 8. Many families find they hold a full day's dishes. (Upper rack alone holds 31 glasses.)

Five modern Colortones, Coppertone, white, or satin-chrome finish. 24-inch undercounter models, maple-top mobile models, and 48-inch dishwasher-sinks. See the new Hotpoint Dishwashers soon!

A Decade of Change for the United Kingdom

Now just imagine you flashed back to a town
in 1956 United Kingdom or Western Europe.

Unlike boom-time America, a very different
picture would await you.

Many major cities like London bore the brunt of destruction from
WWII bombings. The rebuilding process required major loans from the
USA and other nations, leaving the UK heavily in long-term debt. Post-
war Brits were forced to tighten their collective belts, through austerity
measures imposed on everything from fabrics to food.

A central London street in the mid-50s.

The mid-50s saw post-war austerity restrictions finally coming to an
end, a great relief for the British populace. Job security and record low
unemployment meant the middle and working classes were feeling
more prosperous and optimistic than they had for a very long time.
Living standards were rising and families had money to spend.

Young adults and teenagers in particular had spare cash for leisure and luxuries. Looking for a new voice, the British youth of the mid 50s turned to American rock 'n' roll music and fashion, giving rise to a distinct youth culture focused on freedom and rebellion.

British teenagers at a party.

Lack of excess cash reserves made it increasing difficult for the UK to continue financing and keeping secure its far-flung colonies. As a result, many British colonies would be released in the following 10 years, gaining independence as new nations. The United Kingdom was losing its super-power status on the world's stage.

Strato-Streak V-8 + Strato-Flight Hydra-Matic
Born to Go Together!

Wheeling this big beauty down the road you're in command of a *very special* kind of performance–reserved exclusively for Pontiac owners!

Why so special? Well, first of all, there's the industry's most advanced high-torque, high-compression engine–the brilliant new 227-h.p. Strato-Streak V-8. Most cars would be satisfied to stop right there–but not Pontiac! A new transmission was developed to refine all that power oil-smooth–and refined it is. With Strato-Flight Hydra-Matic, tailor-made for Strato-Streak power–*and nothing else!*

The result? America's newest, smoothest, most modern performance team giving you *the greatest "go" on wheels!*

Why not take up your Pontiac dealer's invitation to try it? And ask him about prices. When you do, you and Pontiac will be going steady!

Kissin' Cousin of the Thunderbird

Thunderbird looks, this Ford has aplenty. And it has the mighty Thunderbird Y-8, too. All this, plus new Lifeguard Design!

When the '56 Ford turns on the charm, you'll find it hard to resist.

Ford not only has the heart-winning lines of its Thunderbird cousin, it also has the Thunderbird's famous Y-8 engine. This is the standard eight in all Fairlane and Station Wagon Fords . . . at *no* extra cost!

As for safety, only Ford brings you Lifeguard Design—for added protection against accident injuries. A new deep-center steering wheel, new double-grip door latches, a new shatter-resistant rear-view mirror are standard in all '56 Fords. Ford also offers optional Lifeguard instrument panel and sun visor padding, and seat belts. Come in and Test Drive a '56 Ford now!

'56 Ford ...the *fine* car at half the fine car price!

Thunderbird looks, this Ford has aplenty. And it has the mighty Thunderbird Y-8, too. All this, plus new Lifeguard Design!

When the '56 Ford turns on the charm, you'll find it hard to resist.

Ford not only has the heart-winning lines of its Thunderbird's cousin, it also has the Thunderbird's famous Y-8 engine. This is the standard eight in all Fairlane and Station Wagon Fords... at *no* extra cost!

As for safety, only Ford brings you Lifeguard Design—for added protection against accident injuries. A new deep-center steering wheel, new double-grip door latches, a new shatter-resistant rear-view mirror are standard in all '56 Fords. Ford also offers optional Lifeguard instrument panel and sun visor padding, and seat belts. Come in and Test Drive a '56 Ford now!

'56 Ford... the *fine* car at half the fine car price!

Our Love Affair with Cars

By 1956, the US dominated the world's car market, producing more than half of all new vehicles. In just ten years, the car industry had shifted from fabricating utilitarian war tanks and trucks, to producing fashionable consumer vehicles, the kind of which we just had to have.

There were now 54 million registered cars on US roads, up from 28 million ten years earlier.[1] Rising incomes meant the car was no longer considered a luxury reserved only for the wealthy. Our love affair with cars had begun.

Customers select from a range of cars on display.

Teenagers at a drive-through in the 50s.

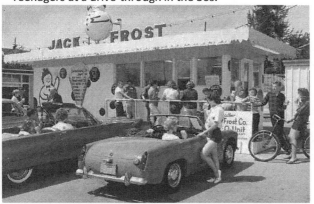

Services related business such as drive-through restaurants and drive-in cinemas were springing up everywhere, especially popular among the younger generation.

[1] fhwa.dot.gov/ohim/summary95/mv200.pdf.

Our love affair with cars grew hand-in-hand with the post-war baby boom and housing construction boom. Where would we be without our cars? How else could we get from our suburban homes to our downtown offices?

Car manufacturers competed for our attention with stylish designs, larger engines, and added detailing. The rising middle classes had money to spend, and cars became the ultimate status symbol.

Craftsmanship

with a flair!

Studebaker THE BIG NEW CHOICE IN THE LOW PRICE FIELD

Cars were no longer just a necessity; they had become an expression of our personality. Sturdy, sporty, or luxurious, cars now came in a wide range of styles, colors, and price-points. Decorative chrome and tail fins reached new heights as the decade progressed, with flamboyant wings and stripes for added pizzazz.

To satisfy the 50s consumer desire for style over efficiency and safety, American car manufacturers produced year-on-year bigger, longer and heavier gas-guzzlers. However, by the end of the decade consumers would begin turning against this extravagance and excess.

Queen of the SHOW ... *and the road!*

The dashing new Chevrolet Bel Air. One of 19 new Chevrolet models all with the distinctive style and quality of famous Fisher Body.

Five car-producing countries dominated the industry by the start of 1956: England, France, Germany and Italy, with America in the top spot. (Japan had yet to enter this elite group.)

Greater performance than ever!

presents the new '56

Austin-Healey 100

The New MG Ⓐ

The safest, fastest MG ever engineered!

command. Driver and motor car become one, in a thrilling partnership of road mastery.

PORSCHE
1600 s.c. COUPE
luxuriously hand-finished
sports touring model.
$3480
FOB New York.

Other Porsche models
from $3076
FOB New York.

PORSCHE

Left: MGA by MG, 1955-56.
Top: Austin Healey 100, 1956.
Below: Porsche 1600, 1956.

America's automotive industry was the largest industry segment in the country, and Detroit was America's car manufacturing powerhouse. The "the Big Three" (General Motors, Ford and Chrysler), all based in the Detroit area, dominated the industry, selling 94% of all US cars during the years 1955-1956.

GM Chevrolet assembly line, 1955.

By the end of the decade Detroit would become the 4th largest city in the US. A whopping one in six American adults would be employed in the car industry nation-wide.[1]

[1] theweek.com/articles/461968/rise-fall-detroit-timeline.

Owners tell us that one of the most rewarding aspects of Cadillac ownership is the remarkable *friendliness* which they encounter at the wheel. Wherever they travel, they find that the "car of cars" introduces them in a very special manner—and seems to inspire the confidence and respect of those about them. This unique Cadillac virtue comes, of course, as something extra when you make your decision for Cadillac. It comes in addition to the car's great and inspiring beauty—its outstanding performance—and its marvelous comfort and handling ease. We suggest that you stop in for a personal appraisal of this glorious list of Cadillac virtues—and to learn why this is such a wonderful season to make the move, both for delivery and economy.

Your Cadillac Dealer

JAN 5 PHILCO AUTOMATIC TOP TOUCH TUNING

NEVER BEFORE LESS THAN $289.95 NOW YOURS

BRAND NEW FOR ONLY $199.95 A BIG $90 LESS FOR

THE ONLY PHOTO-PERFECT TV THAT TUNES ITSELF

AT THESE NEW LOW PRICES DON'T SETTLE FOR LESS THAN A PHILCO

Touch! there's your station

REMOTE CONTROL optional . . . change stations from clear across the room!

PHILCO automatic
Top Touch Tuning

No wonder the demands for Philco Automatic Top Touch Tuning have hit landslide proportions! It's the one modern, up-to-date way to enjoy television at its finest. Just a touch turns the set on. A touch changes stations. A touch turns it off. It's *all automatic* and only Philco has it. Now you can own a new '56 Philco, built to shatter all performance records and complete with automatic Top Touch Tuning for $90 less than before!

PHILCO. *Famous for Quality the World Over*

Philco 4033. Diagonally Measured 21-inch Photo-Perfect TV. Automatic Top Touch Tuning Now at a Record Breaking $19995

Jan 5 Philco Automatic Top Touch Tuning
Never before less than $289.95 now yours
Brand new for only $199.99. A big $90 less for
the only photo-perfect tv that tunes itself
At these new low prices don't settle for less than a Philco

No wonder the demands for Philco Automatic Top Touch Tuning have hit landslide proportions! It's the one modern, up-to-date way to enjoy television at its finest. Just a touch turns the set on. A touch changes stations. A touch turns it off. It's *all automatic* and only Philco has it. Now you can own a new '56 Philco, built to shatter all performance records and complete with automatic Top Touch Tuning for $90 less than before!

Philco. *Famous for Quality the World Over.*

Tuning in to Television

A typical family watching television in the mid 50s.

Taking pride of place in our lounge-rooms, 72% of US households owned a television set by 1956.[1] For the rising middle classes, television had become our preferred means of entertainment.

The early to mid 50s is fondly referred to as the first "Golden Age of Television". During this time, live broadcasts from New York City dominated TV primetime. Based on radio and the theatrical traditions of Broadway, these shows were cheap and quick to produce.

However by 1956, the newer formats produced out of Los Angeles were gaining in popularity—sitcoms, soap operas, westerns, quiz shows, crime and medical dramas would soon become our primetime staples.

The big Hollywood film studios, having lost much of their viewing public to television, now sought profitable ways to enter the small screen business.

Warner Brothers, MGM and 20th Century Fox invested heavily in made-for-TV shows. And by the end of the decade, TV primetime would be dominated by Hollywood produced programs.

Natalie Wood and Gig Young in *Warner Brothers Presents* (ABC. 1955-1956).

[1] americancentury.omeka.wlu.edu/items/show/136.

Most Popular TV Shows of 1956

1	I Love Lucy	11	Dragnet
2	The Ed Sullivan Show	12	Arthur Godfrey's Talent Scouts
3	General Electric Theater	13	The Millionaire
4	The $64,000 Question	=	Disneyland
5	December Bride	15	The Red Skelton Show
6	Alfred Hitchcock Presents	=	The Lineup
7	I've Got a Secret	17	You Bet Your Life
=	Gunsmoke	18	The Life and Legend of Wyatt Earp
9	The Perry Como Show	19	The Ford Show
10	The Jack Benny Show	20	The Adventures of Robin Hood

* From the Nielsen Media Research 1956-57 season of top-rated primetime television series.

I Love Lucy was Lucille Ball's first foray into television and cemented her career as one of comedy's all-time greats. During the show's six-season run, it remained the most watched TV show in the US for four years. Ball co-produced the show with her real-life husband Desi Arnaz.

Lucille Ball with Orson Welles in
I Love Lucy (CBS. 1951-1957).

Long before he was President of the USA, Ronald Regan was a well know TV personality. As host and part owner of *General Electric Theater* (CBS. 1953-1962), he became known as "The Great Communicator". It is said he developed his public-speaking skills through the many public forums he was invited to speak at.

Bill Cullen as the host of
The Price is Right (NBC. 1956-1965).

Don MacLaughlin, Eileen Fulton and Helen Wagner
in *As the World Turns* (CBS. 1956-2010).

The television networks were quick to turn out new programs to keep us tuning in. Here are just a few of the new programs that aired for the first time in 1956: *The Price is Right, The Ford Show, The Errol Flynn Theatre, Ethel Barrymore Theatre, The Adventures of Dr. Fu Manchu,* and the long running *As the World Turns (54 seasons),*

Host Tennessee Ernie Ford with guest Charles
Laughton in *The Ford Show* (NBC. 1956-1961).

Glen Gordon and Carla Balenda in
The Adventures of Dr. Fu Manchu (NBC. 1956).

Chun King Cantonese-style Dinner is newest hit in tray meals—a new mood in food

Now get well=loved Cantonese food dished up the modern way!

Aren't those tray dinners fun? Now there's a brand new one! *Chun King Cantonese-style Dinner* brings you an easy meal that's a delightful new mood in food. Three wonderful Cantonese delicacies . . . cooked, frozen, ready to heat and serve in their own tray!

You get a big helping of Chicken Almond Chop Suey . . . fluffy white rice . . . and two crispy Shrimp Egg

Rolls. Chun King quality, so famous in canned foods, now fresh-frozen for new convenience. Also get Chun King Chicken Chow Mein for two, Shrimp Chow Mein and Egg Rolls in your grocer's frozen food cabinet.

CHUN KING

The Royalty of American-Oriental Foods

Chun King Cantonese-styled Dinner is newest hit in tray meals—a new mood in food

Now get well-loved Cantonese food dished up the modern way!

Aren't those tray dinners fun? Now there's a brand new one! *Chun King Cantonese-style Dinner* brings you an easy meal that's a delightful new mood in food. Three wonderful Cantonese delicacies... cooked, frozen, ready to heat and serve in their own tray!

You get a big helping of Chicken Almond Chop Suey... fluffy white rice... and two crispy Shrimp Egg Rolls. Chun King quality, so famous in canned foods, now fresh-frozen for new convenience. Also get Chun King Chicken Chow Mein for two, Shrimp Chow Mein and Egg Rolls in your grocer's frozen food cabinet.

Chun King
The Royalty of American-Oriental Foods

Billed as the largest public works project in the history of America, the *National Interstate and Defense Highways Act* of 1956 was signed into law by President Dwight D. Eisenhower on 29th June 1956. The ambitious project planned to construct 41,000 miles (66,000 km) of interstate highways over a ten-year period.

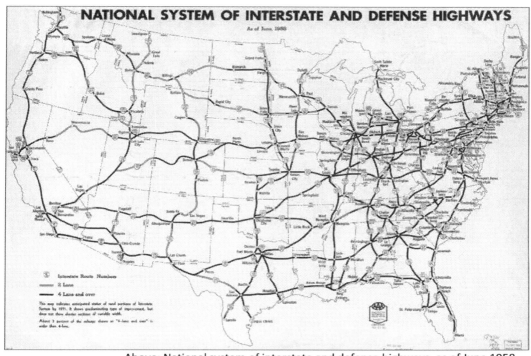

Above: National system of interstate and defense highways, as of June 1958.
Below: Missouri claims the first interstate highway project to begin construction.

The Act addressed the woefully inadequate network of local and national highways. It aimed to reduce death and injury caused by unsafe roads, reduce traffic jams, provide for smoother and more efficient transportation of goods, and to prepare the nation for "catastrophe or defense, should an atomic war come." [1]

[1] From the speech to State Governors, prepared by President Eisenhower and delivered by Vice President Richard M. Nixon at Lake George, NY, 12th July 1954.

Stalking wild game with Parliaments? A risky bit, Sahib. Even with the new 85-millimeter *King Size!*
Yet some smokers go surprisingly far to let everyone know there's something special about Parliaments. And you, too, will appreciate
the crush-proof cigarette case . . . the superb tobaccos . . . the luxurious flavor . . . and above all, the exclusive Mouthpiece
that keeps the filter deeply recessed away from your lips. With Parliaments, *only the flavor touches your lips!*

You're so smart to smoke Parliaments

ONLY THE FLAVOR ... TOUCHES YOUR LIPS

Stalking wild game with Parliaments? A risky bit, Sahib. Even with the new 85-millimeter King Size! Yet some smokers go surprisingly far to let everyone know there's something special about Parliaments. And you, too, will appreciate the crush-proof cigarette case... the superb tobaccos... the luxurious flavor... and above all, the exclusive Mouthpiece that keeps the filter deeply recessed away from your lips. With Parliaments, *only the flavor touches your lips!*

You're so smart to smoke Parliaments

Montgomery Bus Boycott Ends 20th December 1956

On 20th December 1956, a 381-day bus boycott by African American commuters and their supporters, ended with a Supreme Court ruling banning racial segregation on Montgomery buses.

Led by a young Dr. Martin Luther King jr., the Montgomery Bus Boycott is regarded as the first large scale civil rights protest in the USA.

The boycott began in Dec 1955, when 42-year-old activist Rosa Parks was arrested on a Montgomery bus for refusing to give up her seat to a white passenger. During Park's trial 4 days later, 500 supporters came to the court-house, while a further 40,000 commuters boycotted the buses, car pooling or walking to work.

Left, top to bottom: Rosa Parks with Dr. Martin Luther King jr. 1955.
Parks riding a bus, 1956.
Parks being fingerprinted by police, 1956.

The No. 2857 bus on which Parks was riding before her arrest, exhibited at the Henry Ford Museum in Detroit MI. Statues of Parks' sitting on a bus at the National Civil Rights Museum in Memphis TN, and in the United States Capitol.

Parks continued fighting for equality throughout her long and prolific life.

When she died on 24th October 2005, she became the first woman, and the second African American, to lie in honor in the US State Rotunda.

The British Clean Air Act

Aerial view of Big Ben and Houses of Parliament during the Great Smog of 1952 (top image) and on a clear day 2013.

Four years after London saw the deaths of up to 12,000 people from the Great Smog of 1952, the *Clean Air Act* of 1956 was signed into law.

By placing the health of British citizens above business profits and economic concerns, the Clean Air Act marked a turning point in political environmental thought.

The Act mandated smokeless zones where gas or electric heating would replace coal-burning fires. Heavy industry and power stations would be moved out of cities and required to install tall chimney stacks with pollutant scrubbers.

The Great Smog of 1952 saw London blanketed in a heavy fog, laden with sulphur dioxide and other industrial pollutants. An unusual high-pressure anticyclone kept the lethal smog trapped at ground level over London for a full five days.

Visibility was so poor that people couldn't see their own feet. Trains and traffic came to a stand still. Hospitals filled with patients suffering from bronchitis and pneumonia.

Big Ben seen during the Great Smog, 1952.

In 1968 and 1970, new UK Clean Air Acts further strengthened the Act of 1956, specifically targeting hydrocarbons and carbon monoxide from automobiles. The revised acts put pressure on car manufacturers to strenuously reduce their toxic emissions.

For the USA and other industrialized countries, similar legislation on air quality would not come into effect for many years.

The US introduced its first Clean Air Act in 1963, although it did little to combat air pollution. The revised Clean Air Act of 1970 was the first to set clear requirements on pollution reduction.

New York aerial view in 1973 and now.

L.A. Grand Avenue in 1967 and now.

In Canada, Australia, and across Europe, similar legislations were developed throughout the 70s to tackle the undeniable problem of automobile-created photochemical smog which affected all major cities.

Every country set their own standards, some more stringent than others. They also created their own methods for emissions testing of vehicles prior to sale, and of air quality testing for cities.

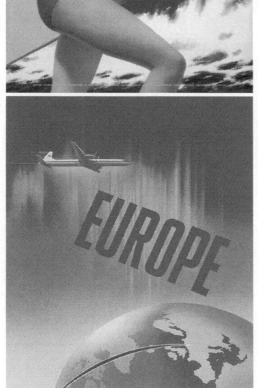

Vintage Airline Posters from 1956.

No. 10 in a new series:

This "Big Stick" stops trouble *before it starts*

So powerful that it revises infantry strategy, the Douglas *Honest John* is an artillery rocket of tremendous destructive force and deadly accuracy.

Designed and built by Douglas Aircraft, Honest John moves into position on its own launching truck. This free-flight missile can carry the heaviest high explosive charge, or an atomic warhead in weather that grounds tactical air cover. Its very existence deters an enemy from massing for effective ground attack.

HONEST JOHN puts a mobile atomic weapon up front with the infantry

Development of Honest John by Douglas engineers fills a vital infantry need and provides new muscle for our armed forces. But the basic strength of any defense depends on people. Find out what an important future there is for *you* in U. S. Army service.

Depend on *DOUGLAS*   First in Aviation

This "Big Stick" stops trouble before it starts

So powerful that it revises infantry strategy, the Douglas *Honest John* is an artillery rocket of tremendous destructive force and deadly accuracy.

Designed and built by Douglas Aircraft, Honest John moves into position on its own launching truck. This free-flight missile can carry the heaviest high explosive charge, or an atomic warhead in weather that grounds tactical air cover. Its very existence deters an enemy from massing for effective ground attack.

Honest John puts a mobile atomic weapon in front with the infantry.

Development of Honest John by Douglas engineers fills a vital infantry need and provides new muscle for our armed forces. But the basic strength of any defense depends on people. Find out what an important future there is for *you* in U.S. Army Service.

The Cold War–Nuclear Arms Race

Cold War tensions between the two former allies–the USSR and the USA–continued from post war 1945 until 1991.

Starting in the USA as policies for communist containment, the distrust and misunderstanding between the two sides quickly escalated from political squabbling to a military nuclear arms race. Trillions of dollars in military spending saw both sides stockpile nuclear arsenals, strategically positioning their missiles to point directly at each other.

The superpowers also raced to develop more powerful bombs and longer reaching missiles. The USA tested its first hydrogen bomb in 1954, with the USSR testing theirs in 1955.

By 1956, the US Air Force had begun developing a long range intercontinental ballistic missile, capable of delivering a nuclear weapon. The following year the Soviets confirmed they had successfully developed long range missiles able to reach any corner of the earth.

USA ballistic missile ready to launch, 1955.

Warhead statistics from 1956 show the USA had a stockpile of 3692 nuclear weapons, against the Soviet's 426 weapons.[1] Both sides continued to increase their stockpiles. American stockpiles peaked in 1967 with a total of 31,225 against the Soviet's 8,339 weapons.[1]

The USSR continued to grow their stockpile until 1988, after which the two superpowers ended the Nuclear Arms Race with the signing of a denuclearization treaty in 1991.

[1] tandfonline.com/doi/pdf/10.2968/066004008.

The Hungarian Revolution
23rd Oct–4th Nov 1956

It began as a peaceful student uprising on the streets of Budapest. On 23rd October 1956, 200,000 students and their supporters marched to the Hungarian Parliament demanding a more open and democratic political system, while rejecting the Soviet inspired communism that the ruling Hungarian Working People's Party had installed.

Crowd cheers Hungarian troops in Budapest.

As the night drew on, fearful of the protest's escalation, the People's Party Secretary called for Soviet assistance. By noon the following day, Soviet tanks and soldiers surrounded Budapest, barricading key buildings, bridges and crossroads.

Soviet tanks abandoned in Budapest, Oct 1956.

Over the next few days as many as 70 armed clashes broke out across the country. The attacks forced the collapse of the ruling government. More than 200 of its members were lynched or executed while the Prime Minister fled to Moscow. 8,000 political prisoners were released.

The revolutionaries enjoyed a short-lived success, installing a new National Government, demanding the immediate withdrawal of Soviet troops, and the country's withdrawal from the Warsaw Pact. However, on 4th November, the Soviets sent 17 armed divisions into Budapest to forcefully crush the uprising. Thousands were killed in the violent clashes. More than 200,000 civilians fled the country.

Crisis on the Suez Canal 26ᵗʰ Jul–22ⁿᵈ Dec 1956

Carved out of the Egyptian desert sands in the mid-19ᵗʰ century, the Suez Canal connected the Mediterranean Sea to the Red Sea, thereby reducing shipping times from Europe to Asia Pacific by as much as 8 to 10 days.

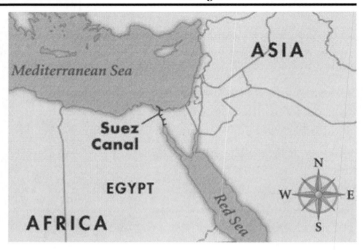

A joint French-Egyptian company had been created to construct the canal– The Suez Canal Company. They maintained the right to operate the canal for 99 years. However, a mere 6 years after opening, financial troubles forced the Egyptians to sell their shares to the British.

On 26ᵗʰ July 1956, Egyptian President Gamal Abdel Nasser nationalized the canal, seizing control of The Suez Canal Company, to access much-needed funds raised through ship tolls. At the same time, Nasser ordered a ban on all Israeli ships from passage through the canal. The Suez Crisis had begun.

The United Kingdom and France plotted with Israel to regain control of the canal. First Israel invaded, engaging Egyptian forces in battle. The British and French argued that the military attacks threatened the stability of the Middle East. This gave them a valid reason to enter the war.

Crew of an Israeli Defense Force jeep waving at a French Air Force Bomber, Nov 1956.

British and French troops invaded the region on 31st October, just two days after the Israeli invasion. The allies quickly destroyed the Egyptian army.

Smoke rises from oil tanks beside the Suez Canal hit during the initial Anglo-French assault on Port Said, 5th Nov 1956.

Nassar responded by blocking the canal, sinking or trapping 47 ships within. The canal would not open again until March 1957.

The invasion enraged the world's superpowers, with the USSR threatening to enter the conflict. Fearing another Cold War battlefront, the USA demanded an immediate cessation of hostilities. Bowing to pressure, British and French troops withdrew in December 1956. The Suez Crisis ended with the Israeli withdrawal in early 1957.

In 1967 Israel engaged in battle with Egypt a second time over the use of the Suez Canal. The ensuing war saw the canal closed for 8 years.

More recently, the Suez Canal closed from 23rd - 29th March 2021 when the Ever Given ran aground diagonally, causing delays to more than 200 awaiting vessels. It was the third time a ship had veered off course and blocked the canal.

Container Ship 'Ever Given' stuck in the Suez Canal, Egypt - 24th March 2021.

Cine-Kodak K-100 Turret Camera, f/1.9, $315.
Extra-long film run. Speeds from 16 to 64 frames.
Accepts any 5 Ektar Lenses; matching viewfinders.
Kodascope Pageant Sound Projector, 7K4, $459.
For the very finest in 16mm sound or silent movies.

Cine-Kodak Royal Magazine Camera, f/1.9,
$179.50. 3-second loading. 3 speeds. Ektar 25mm
Lens interchanges with telephotos or wide-angle.
Kodascope Royal Projector, $275. Brilliant, quiet,
and so simple—for top 16mm silent shows.

The happiest gifts come from Kodak!

Fine movie cameras and projectors
can save all your happy moments
—in action and color!

If it's made
by Kodak—
you know
it's good!

Brownie Movie Camera, Turret f/1.9, $79.50.
Completely equipped for all three views: regular,
wide-angle, and telephoto. 8mm film economy, too.
Cine-Kodak Showtime 8 Projector, $115. 8mm
movies at their best. "Stills"; reverse-action, too.

*Prices include Federal Tax where applicable and
are subject to change without notice*

Ask your Kodak dealer about convenient terms

EASTMAN KODAK COMPANY
Rochester 4, N.Y.

Kodak
TRADE-MARK

The happiest gifts come from Kodak!

Fine movie cameras and projectors can save all your happy moments—in action and color! If it's made by Kodak—you know it's good!

Cine-Kodak K-100 Turret Camera, f/1.9, $315. Extra-long film run. Speeds from 16 to 64 frames. Accepts any 3 Ektar Lenses; matching viewfinders.
Kodascope Pageant Sound Projector, 7K4, $459. For the very finest in 16mm sound or silent movies.

Cine-Kodak Royal Magazine Camera, f/1.9, $179.50. 3-second loading. 3 speeds. Ektar 25mm Lens interchanges with telephotos or wide-angle.
Kodascope Royal Projector, $275. Brilliant, quiet, and so simple—for top 16mm silent shows.

Brownie Movie Camera, Turret f/1.9, $79.50. Completely equipped for all three views: regular, wide-angle, and telephoto. 8mm film economy, too.
Cine-Kodak Showtime 8 Projector, $115. 8mm movies at their best. "Stills"; reverse-action, too.

Ask your Kodak dealer about convenient terms.

Only Pan American has crossed the Atlantic more than 50,000 times!

It's nice to know "Uncle Sam's" your skipper when you fly to faraway places

No country in the world has requirements of airline operation more strict than those of the U.S. Government. And when you fly Pan Am, it's reassuring to know that Uncle Sam's rules are met *with a generous margin to spare* by the only U.S. airline serving 78 countries and colonies around the world.

PAN AMERICAN

WORLD'S MOST EXPERIENCED AIRLINE

Only Pan American has crossed the Atlantic more than 50,000 times!

It's nice to know "Uncle Sam's" your skipper when you fly to faraway places.

No country in the world has requirements of airline operation more strict than those of the U.S. Government. And when you fly Pan Am, it's reassuring to know that Uncle Sam's rules are met *with a generous margin to spare* by the only U.S. airline serving 78 countries and colonies around the world.

Pan American
World's most experienced airline

Cinema and Films of 1956

Kim Novak & James Stewart in *Vertigo,* 1958.

Highest Paid Stars

1 William Holden
2 John Wayne
3 James Stewart
4 Burt Lancaster
5 Glenn Ford
6 Dean Martin
= Jerry Lewis
8 Marilyn Monroe
9 Gary Cooper
10 Kim Novak

With television becoming ever more commonplace in American homes, cinema attendance faced a steady decline throughout the 1950s. In order to win over new audiences, the motion picture industry sought the attention of younger viewers who had more leisure time and cash to spare.

The mid 50s brought a new wave of exciting, young, sexy, anti-hero stars, such as Marlon Brando, James Dean, Kim Novak, Marilyn Monroe and Paul Newman.

Dean Martin, Jerry Lewis and Marilyn Monroe, at the 1953 Redbook Awards.

Elvis on stage, in 1956.

1956 film debuts

Michael Caine	Panic in the Parlor
Glenda Jackson	The Extra Day
Joan Plowright	Moby Dick
Elvis Presley	Love Me Tender
Maggie Smith	Child in the House
Robert Vaughn	The Ten Commandments

* From en.wikipedia.org/wiki/1956_in_film.

Top Grossing Films of 1956

1	The Ten Commandments	Paramount	$10,000,000
2	Around the World in 80 Days	United Artists	$8,500,000
3	Giant	Warner Bros.	$8,100,000
4	Seven Wonders of the World	CRC	$7,100,000
5	The King and I	20th Century Fox	$6,801,000
6	Trapeze	United Artists	$6,500,000
7	War and Peace	Paramount	$6,300,000
8	High Society	MGM	$6,200,000
9	Strategic Air Command	MGM	$6,000,000
10	The Eddy Duchin Story	Columbia Pictures	$6,000,000

* From en.wikipedia.org/wiki/1956_in_film by box office gross in the USA.

Yul Brynner starred as King Mongkut in the film version of *The King and I*, a role he would also play 4,625 times on stage.

Giant was the third and last movie for 24-year-old James Dean. He would die in a head-on car collision before the films release.

A Decade of Cinema Epics

The 1950s saw cinema studios take big risks with extravagant and spectacular epic films. Exotic locations, expensive sets, multiple A-list actors and casts of thousands ensured big ticket sales at the box office.

The biblical epic *The Ten Commandments* portrayed the story of Moses with Charlton Heston in the lead role. Cecil B. DeMille narrated, produced and directed the film, aided by 88 assistant directors. The cast included 14,000 extras and 15,000 animals.

Nominated for seven Academy Awards, the film received an Oscar for *Best Visual Effects*. The parting of the Red Sea was considered the most difficult special effect ever produced, taking six months to film.

Charlton Heston as Moses in *The Ten Commandments* (Paramount, 1956).

The historical drama *War and Peace,* based on Leo Tolstoy's 1869 novel of the same name, opened to mixed reviews. Of primary concern was the film's concentration on the central love triangle, while simplifying the book's multiple plot lines. 50-year-old Henry Fonda was also considered too old for the role of 20-year-old Pierre.

Audrey Hepburn, one of Hollywood's biggest stars at the time, played the lead role of Natasha for a record $350,000. Hepburn secured the role of Andrei for her then real-life husband Mel Ferrer.

On the set of *War and Peace,* (above) Audrey Hepburn as Natasha, and Mel Ferrer as Andrei. (Below) Henry Fonda as Pierre, Anita Ekberg as Hélène, with Mel Ferrer (Paramount, 1956).

Around the World in 80 Days swept up at the Academy Awards, taking home five Oscars including *Best Picture* and *Best Cinematography*. Based on the 1873 Jules Verne novel of the same name, the epic adventure-comedy film starred A-listers David Niven, Shirley MacLaine, Robert Newton, and Mexican superstar Cantinflas.

Filming took place at break-neck speed across 13 countries throughout Europe, England, Asia and America. A total of 140 sets were specialty built on location.

More than 60,000 extras were engaged to fill the many crowd scenes. In the small Spanish town of Chinchón, the entire population of 6,500 residents was hired to fill the bull-fight stadium.

Movie poster for *Around the World in 80 days* (United Artists, 1956).

To add to the mayhem, nearly 8,000 live animals joined the actors. Elephants, ostriches, monkeys and fighting bulls were just some of the exotic animals on set, along with many thousands of sheep, donkeys and wild buffalo, requiring ninety specialist animal handlers.

The film also boasted over 40 cameos by major film stars, including Frank Sinatra, Marlene Dietrich, Red Skelton and Buster Keaton.

Film crew with elephants in Bangladesh, 1955.

Robert Newton, David Niven, Mario Moreno and Cantinflas on set.

No. 11 in a series:

Sprints from deck to stratosphere

His beat is the oceans of the world. His job, to challenge unknown intruders on our defense perimeters. A Navy pilot is a seagoing sentry on 24-hour duty.

A major role in this job of positive interception—and as far from our shores as possible—is being assigned to the Douglas F4D Skyray. Less than a minute after leaving the deck, Skyray can soar past the 10,000-ft. mark. Seconds later it's hissing through the stratosphere . . . 35,000 feet up . . . at the ready with rockets and cannons.

This rate of climb comes as no surprise. Skyray also holds the world's official F.A.I. sea level speed records for the 3- and 100-kilometre courses.

Douglas F4D Skyray—fastest carrier-based interceptor. Performance of agile Skyray continues the Douglas tradition of "faster and farther with a bigger payload." Yet performance figures are meaningless without a skilled pilot at the controls. If you are interested in a career as a Naval Aviator, write Nav. Cad. Washington 25, D. C.

Depend on *DOUGLAS*   First in Aviation

Sprints from deck to stratosphere

His beat is the oceans of the world. His job, to challenge unknown intruders on our defense perimeters. A Navy pilot is a seagoing sentry on 24-hour duty.

A major role in this job of positive interception–and as far from our shores as possible–is being assigned to the Douglas F4D Skyray. Less than a minute after leaving the deck, Skyray can soar past the 10,000-ft. mark. Seconds later it's hissing through the stratosphere... 35,000 feet up... at the ready with rockets and cannons.

This rate of climb comes as no surprise. Skyray also holds the world's official F.A.I. sea level speed records for the 3- and 100- kilometre courses.

Douglas F4D Skyray–fastest carrier-based interceptor. Performance of agile Skyray continues the Douglas tradition of "faster and farther with a bigger payload." Yet performance figures are meaningless without a skilled pilot at the controls. If you are interested in a career as a Naval Aviator, write Nav. Cad. Washington 25, D.C.

Depend on Douglas – First in Aviation.

No...
the IBM Electric
can't decipher
shorthand
but...

...it will give you the world's most eye-catching
letters—and increase office efficiency, too!

Letters are handsomer, easier to read when they're typed on the IBM Electric! Whatever touch a typist uses, she always gets uniform, "letter-perfect" typing.

Less time, less effort—because the IBM Electric requires 95.4% less "finger-effort" than a manual. Ease of operation

and the many IBM time-saving aids help get typing done in far less time.

Increases efficiency because the IBM helps handle more work without added secretarial expense. Remember, the IBM costs no more than other electrics... and pays for itself fast! Call IBM today.

IBM ELECTRIC TYPEWRITERS

Available in these
8 handsome colors

—OUTSELL ALL OTHER ELECTRICS COMBINED!

No... the IBM Electric <u>can't</u> decipher shorthand but...
...it <u>will</u> give you the world's most eye-catching letters—
and increase office efficiency, too!

Letters are handsomer, easier to read when they're typed on the IBM Electric! Whatever touch a typist uses, she always get uniform, "letter-perfect" typing.

Less time, less effort—because the IBM Electric requires 95.4% less "finger-effort" than a manual. Ease of operation and the many IBM time-saving aids help get typing done in *far less time*.

Increases efficiency because the IBM helps handle *more* work without added secretarial expense. Remember, the IBM costs no more than other electrics... and pays for itself *fast!* Call IBM today.

IBM Electric Typewriters – outsell all other electrics combined!

My Fair Lady Broadway Triumph

Julie Andrews and Rex Harrison (with Robert Coote) in *My Fair Lady* original Broadway production.

My Fair Lady opened on Broadway's Mark Hellinger Theater on 15th March 1956 to triumphant reviews. It would run for 6 years, the longest continuous running show at that time. The show caused a sensation at the Tony Awards the following year, winning 7 of its 11 nominations including *Best Musical*. The crowd pleaser was equally triumphant when it opened on London's West End in 1958.

The original Broadway cast starred a young Julie Andrews as Eliza Doolittle, and Rex Harrison as Henry Higgins. Both would reprise their roles on the West End, where the show ran for 5 years.

My Fair Lady has since been staged in countless cities world-wide and seen numerous revivals. The critically acclaimed film version, also starring Rex Harrison, was released in 1964.

Although Andrews was perfect for the character of Eliza Doolittle, she had yet to star in a major Hollywood film and was overlooked for the role in the 1964 film version. Audrey Hepburn was selected for the lead. Hepburn, an A-list actress at the time, was not a singer. All her songs were dubbed by studio ghost singer Marni Nixon. (Nixon also dubbed for Deborah Kerr in *The King and I*, and Natalie Wood in *West Side Story*).

Julie Andrews on stage with original cast members.

Publicity photo of Audrey Hepburn for *My Fair Lady*, 1964.

My Fair Lady was created as an adaption of the 1913 play *Pygmalion* by George Bernard Shaw. It set a new standard for musical theater, with its perfect balance of singing, dancing and drama.

Columbia Records President Goddard Lieberson personally financed the $375,000 needed to bring the show to Broadway, in exchange for the rights in perpetuity to the original cast album.

It Defies
Comparison!

**THE ROYAL "500"
POCKET RADIO**

Only 3½" wide, 5¼" high,
1½" deep. 19 ounces.
Two colors: black (500Y)
or maroon (500R) both
with Roman gold trim.
Case: Unbreakable nylon.
$75.00*

Jack for silent
earphone attachment.

7 transistors. Not just 4 or 5,
but 7 to give you the very best
performance in pocket radios!

Up to 15 times more volume
than radios of equivalent size and...

Up to 30 times more sensitivity
to bring in more distant stations

Up to 400 hours battery life
from one set of mercury batteries!
Like filling your car with gas only
twice a year!

Announcing Zenith's New Tubeless Pocket Radio

So powerful it plays on trains, boats and planes where others won't!

THIS superb new Zenith radio— the 7-transistor Royal "500"—is so powerful it actually operates where others won't... gives clear reception indoors, outdoors or in a car. Just think! You no longer need both a car radio and a portable! The Royal "500", with its unbreakable nylon case, gives you both!

And here's more good news! It operates for only a *fraction of a cent* an hour on the new long-lasting mercury batteries (up to 400 hours), or on inexpensive penlite batteries, available everywhere.

When you see the beautiful Royal "500" at your Zenith dealer's, we think you'll agree it's the finest pocket radio you've ever seen... or heard!

ZENITH THE QUALITY GOES IN
BEFORE THE NAME GOES ON

The Royalty of RADIO and Television
Backed by 37 years of leadership
in radionics exclusively
ALSO MAKERS OF FINE HEARING AIDS
Zenith Radio Corporation, Chicago 39, Ill.

---

7 transistors. Not just 4 or 5, but 7 to give you the very best performance in pocket radios!
Up to 15 times more volume than radios of equivalent size and...
Up to 30 times more sensitivity to bring in more distant stations.
Up to 400 hours battery life from one set of mercury batteries! Like filling your car with gas only twice a year!

Announcing Zenith's New Tubeless Pocket Radio
So powerful it plays on trains, boats and planes where others won't!

This superb new Zenith radio–the 7-transistor Royal "500"–is so powerful it actually operates where others won't... gives clear reception indoors, outdoors or in a car. Just think! You no longer need both a car radio and a portable! The Royal "500", with its unbreakable nylon case, gives you both!

And here's more good news! It operates for only a *fraction of a cent* an hour on new long-lasting mercury batteries (up to 400 hours), or on inexpensive penlite batteries, available everywhere.

When you see the beautiful Royal "500" at your Zenith dealer's, we think you'll agree it's the finest pocket radio you've ever seen... or heard!

Rock 'n' Roll Revolution

Rock 'n' Roll exploded onto our soundwaves in the mid-fifties, and took the world by storm. It burst from the ghettos, from small town local record studios, while the big city record labels were napping. The energy, the rhythm, the emotion—we had never heard anything quite like it before. Parents were alarmed and appalled in equal measure.

Jerry Lee Lewis.

Rock 'n' Roll was the first music ever created specifically for teenagers. The first of the Baby Boomers had found their sound. It was neither black nor white. It gave expression to youth of any race and social status. It was a mash of rhythm & blues, country & western, gospel, hillbilly, blues, and jazz, with a heavy rock beat.

Chuck Berry, Fats Domino, Bill Haley and his Comets, Jerry Lee Lewis, and of course Elvis Presley, became household names.

Sun Records in Memphis TN was home to many rock 'n' roll greats, including Elvis Presley, Jerry Lee Lewis, Carl Perkins, Jonny Cash, Roy Orbison, and Howlin' Wolf.

In Nov 1955, Presley's contract was sold to the giant record label RCA for a massive $40,000.

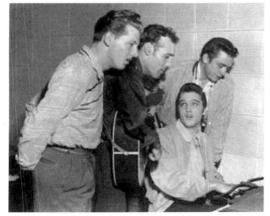

On 4th Dec 1956, Presley dropped by Sun Records, and an impromptu jam session with friends was captured. Known as the "Million Dollar Quartet", sound recordings of Presley with Lewis, Perkins, and Cash were publicly released in 1991.

The Million Dollar Quartet. L-R: Jerry Lee Lewis, Carl Perkins, Elvis Presley and Johnny Cash.

Billboard Top 30 Songs of 1956

	Artist	Song Title
1	Elvis Presley	Heartbreak Hotel
2	Elvis Presley	Don't Be Cruel
3	Nelson Riddle	Lisbon Antigua
4	The Platters	My Prayer
5	Gogi Grant	The Wayward Wind
6	Les Baxter	The Poor People of Paris
7	Doris Day	Que Sera, Sera (Whatever Will Be, Will Be)
8	Elvis Presley	Hound Dog
9	Dean Martin	Memories Are Made of This
10	Kay Starr	(The) Rock and Roll Waltz

The Platters.

Gogi Grant.

Doris Day.

Dean Martin.

	Artist	Song Title
11	Morris Stoloff	Moonglow and Theme from Picnic
12	The Platters	The Great Pretender
13	Pat Boone	I Almost Lost My Mind
14	Elvis Presley	I Want You, I Need You, I Love You
15	Elvis Presley	Love Me Tender
16	Perry Como	Hot Diggity (Dog Ziggity Boom)
17	Eddie Heywood & Hugo Winterhalter	Canadian Sunset
18	Carl Perkins	Blue Suede Shoes
19	Jim Lowe	Green Door
20	The Four Lads	No, Not Much

Pat Boone.

Perry Como.

21	Bill Doggett	Honky Tonk
22	Tennessee Ernie Ford	Sixteen Tons
23	Johnnie Ray	Just Walkin' in the Rain
24	Patti Page	Allegheny Moon
25	Fats Domino	I'm in Love Again
26	Patience and Prudence	Tonight You Belong to Me
27	Gene Vincent	Be-Bop-A-Lula
28	Frankie Lymon and the Teenagers	Why Do Fools Fall in Love
29	The Four Lads	Standing on the Corner
30	Buchanan & Goodman	The Flying Saucer

* From the *Billboard* top 30 singles of 1956.

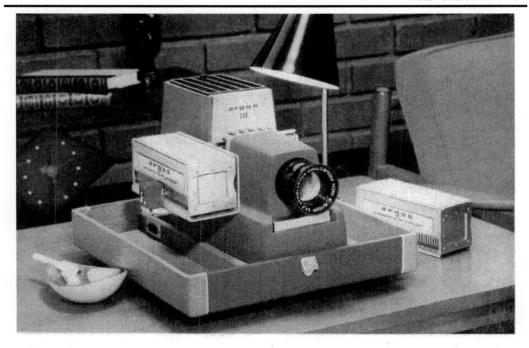

See your color slides in a beautiful new light... *life-size!*

WITH THE NEW ARGUS AUTOMATIC PROJECTOR

complete with carrying case, automatic slide changer, slide editor and 36-slide magazine $59.50

You've photographed the big moments of your life in color. Now relive them again and again—big as life and just as colorful—with this all-new Argus Automatic Projector!

A new, advanced optical system delivers more light through the wide-angle lens to give you pictures uniformly bright and clear, from corner to corner. No dimmed-out edges or "hot" spots.

And your slides are so easy to show. A quick push-pull of the operating handle positions each slide for perfect viewing, returns it to the magazine in order, and automatically advances the next slide.

A convenient new Slide Editor lets you preview slides before you file them in the magazine. And a powerful yet silent blower keeps projector and slides cool—even during the longest showings.

To see your color slides in a beautiful new light, see the all-new Argus line of 300-watt projectors at your dealer's now.

Standard model, with non-automatic operation, $37.50. New Remote-Control Power Unit for any Argus Automatic, runs the show by push-button from anywhere in the room, $24.50.

See your color slides in a beautiful new light... *life-size!*
With the new Argus Automatic Projector

Complete with carrying case, automatic slide charger, slide editor and 36-slide magazine $59.50.

You've photographed the big moments of your life in color. Now relive them again and again—big as life and just as colorful—with this all-new Argus Automatic Projector!

A new, advanced optical system delivers more light through the wide-angle lens to give you pictures uniformly bright and clear, from corner to corner. No dimmed-out edges or "hot" spots.

And your slides are so easy to show. A quick push-pull of the operating handle positions each slide for perfect viewing, returns it to the magazine in order, and automatically advances to the next slide.

A convenient new Slide Editor lets you preview slides before you file them in the magazine. And a powerful yet silent blower keeps projector and slides cool—even during the longest showings.

To see your color slides in a beautiful new light, see the all-new Argus line of 300-watt projectors at your dealer's now.

Standard model, with non-automatic operation, $37.50. New Remote-Control Power Unit for any Argus Automatic, runs the show by push-button from anywhere in the room, $24.50.

A home is only as complete as the knowledge it holds.
Complete yours now with the Encyclopedia Americana.

From air conditioning to television, many of today's homes are furnished with every modern convenience science can provide. But a home can only give its fullest satisfaction when it is also equipped with modern *knowledge*–knowledge that's available in The Encyclopedia Americana.

Such knowledge can give you an understanding of the principles behind the scientific wonders in your home... can answer your children's questions about the kaleidoscopic world in which they are living... can explain for your entire family the facts and reasons behind today's rapid developments in science, industry, government and culture.

The Encyclopedia Americana contains over 60,000 articles on a vast variety of topics and all this information is classified and written so it is easy to find, easy to understand. It is *modern* knowledge, too, because The Americana is *revised annually*. Why not make *your* home fuller, more rewarding with these 30 handsome volumes?

*25,000 pages   * 44,000 cross references   * 10,000 illustrations   * easy-to-use index

Elvis Presley is the King of Rock

Having signed a new record label with RCA in Nashville, Elvis Presley burst onto our collective consciousness in January 1956 with the release of *Heartbreak Hotel*. The song quickly became Presley's first number-one hit.

Presley immediately followed with national TV appearances on *Stage Show* (CBS), and the *Milton Berle Show* (NBC). During his debut performance of *Hound Dog*, Presley momentarily stepped away from the microphone to dance, shocking viewers with his energetic hip grinding and gyrations that would become his trademark moves. The conservative public was outraged, causing a national controversy which decried the singer as "unfit for family viewing".

Presley performs live, Sept 1956.

By August 1956, Presley had three performances booked on CBS' *Ed Sullivan Show*, for which he was paid an astonishing $50,000. Clever camera angles concealed his waist-down gyrations, but the crazed, screaming studio audience helped propel Presley's heart-throb celebrity status, pushing rock 'n' roll into mainstream pop culture.

Presley's performance of his soon-to-be-released single *Love Me Tender* resulted in one million advance orders, making it a gold record prior to its release.

By the end of 1956, five of the top fifteen songs in the Billboard Top 100 belonged to Elvis Presley. Sales of his records accounted for half the sales at RCA.

Presley performing live at the Mississippi-Alabama Fairgrounds in Tupelo, Mississippi, 26th Sept 1956. Local police were aided by 50 National Guardsmen to help control the crowd.

Between 1956 and his death in 1977, Presley gave over 1,000 concert performances. He released over 50 singles, in addition to 25 studio albums and 17 movie soundtrack albums, Presley remains the best-selling solo artist of all time.[1]

In May 1956, Presley signed a seven-year contract with Paramount Pictures. His first film, the musical western *Love Me Tender*, was released in November 1956.

Presley would star in thirty-one feature films during his acting career. Although none were critically acclaimed, they were always successful at the box office.

Presley died suddenly in 1977 following years of prescription drug abuse.

Presley broke the boundaries during racially segregated 50s America. His sound appealed to black and white listeners, crossing several genres. He was posthumously inducted into 5 Music Halls of Fame, including those for Country Music, Gospel Music, and Rockabilly.

Presley continues to rank as one of the highest earning deceased celebrities, in large part due to merchandise sales, tours of his Memphis home *Graceland*, and re-releases of his songs.

[1] edition.cnn.com/2013/08/30/us/elvis-presley-fast-facts/index.html.

Dresses from the Aldens Home Order Catalog, Summer 1956.

1950's Fashion Trends

With the penny-pinching misery and bleakness of the war years behind us, the 1950s were a time to show off. And nowhere was this more apparent than through our fashion choices. The pinched waist look of the late 40s carried throughout the 50s decade. Our clothes allowed us to express beauty, excellence, luxury and extravagance.

Fashion of the 50s was highlighted by a clear gender divide. While women's fashion focussed on femininity and tailored formality, men's fashion embraced the casual and cool of working class daywear.

a **FERNFIELD** *fashion*

By the mid-50s, dresses and skirts reached voluminous proportions, with pleats and folds flaunting an abundance of fabric.

Christian Dior's "New Look" from 1947.

Day wear and evening wear for women on both sides of the Atlantic continued to take its direction from the haute couture salons of Paris. Christian Dior's "New Look", unveiled in 1947, set the standard for the entire decade of the 1950s.

Gone were the boxy tailored jackets with padded shoulders and short skirts. Dior had brought back femininity, with clinched waists, fuller busts and hips, and longer, wider skirts. The emphasis was on abundance.

Christian Dior's "New Look" in 1955.

To achieve this impossible hour-glass figure, corsets and girdles were sold in record numbers. Metal underwire bras made a comeback, and a new form of bra known as the "cathedral bra" or "bullet bra" became popular.

Fabulous Figuring by Formfit, 1956.

Women embraced the femininity of 1950's fashion from head to toe. Hats, scarves, belts, gloves, shoes, stockings, handbags and jewelry were all given due consideration.

Out on the street, no outfit was complete without a full complement of matching accessories.

It's simply <u>wicked</u> what it does for you

WARNER'S
Merry Widow

Care to be daring, darling? To look outright naughty, yet feel downright nice? Then why not give in to that inner whisper, and agree to star in this exciting new vehicle.

You'll get all the best lines... all the admiring looks—in your most demanding clothes. Your entrances? Positively breathtaking. Because Warner's knows every beautiful scene-stealing way to keep you in the center of the stage.

Once you taste the spotlights and applause, you'll never go anywhere *important* without your Merry Widow. Here just two of the famous supporting cast. Try the feeling today! From $3.50 at the nicest stores here and in Canada.

#1311. (*Right*) The fabulous original... for a hand-span waist, a grand-stand look. Cuffs turn down or up. Black or white embroidered nylon and elastic marquisette, $12.50.

#1317. (*Left*) The waist a little easier, the lines a little longer; the bust high, round, and youthful for the newest dresses. Black or white embroidered nylon marquisette. $15.00.

Despite criticisms against the extravagance of the New Look, and arguments that heavy corsets and paddings undermined the freedoms women had won during the war years, the New Look was embraced on both sides of the Atlantic.

Dresses from the Lana Lobell Spring-Summer Catalog, 1956.

Clothing manufacturers produced stylish, ready-to-wear clothes for the masses. Inexpensive versions of Dior's New Look in florals and pretty pastels filled our closets and graced our suburban homes and streets. No longer just for the wealthy, the growing middle classes could now afford to be fashionable. Magazines and mail-order catalogs were sure to keep us informed of the latest in fashion and accessories.

ALL FABRICS FROM MEMBER COMPANIES OF BURLINGTON INDUSTRIES

Wonderful day!

Her first high heels... and Bur-Mil Cameo Nylons

What a grand and glorious feeling... the magic of being grown-up. It's a wonderful day... the beginning of an exciting new life for this young lady—and for her mother and dad, too.

Funny, isn't it, how a new pair of shoes, a nice dress, a trim suit—a very special pair of stockings—can make such a difference in the way a person feels.

Take the sheer delight of this young lady's Bur-Mil Cameo "Dubbelife" hosiery, the most significant development in hosiery in years. Although very sheer, they promise to wear twice as long as other stockings... it's another reason why it pays to look for Burlington Industries triangle—a symbol of quality from the world's leading producer of hosiery, and of all fabrics.

"WOVEN INTO THE LIFE OF AMERICA"

This triangle means you can't buy better quality for the money.

MEMBER COMPANIES OF *Burlington* INDUSTRIES, INC. WRITE TO 1830 BROADWAY, NEW YORK 19, N. Y.
BURLINGTON MILLS · BURLINGTON HOSIERY · PEERLESS WOOLENS · BURLINGTON DECORATIVE FABRICS · GALEY & LORD
PACIFIC · GOODALL · BURLINGTON RIBBONS · MALLINSON · ELY & WALKER · MOORESVILLE · BURLINGTON INTERNATIONAL

Wonderful day! Her first high heels... and Bur-Mil Cameo Nylons

What a grand and glorious feeling... the magic of being grown-up. It's a wonderful day... the beginning of an exciting new life for this young lady—and for her mother and dad, too.

Funny, isn't it, how a new pair of shoes, a nice dress, a trim suit—a very special pair of stockings—can make such a difference in the way a person feels.

Take the sheer delight of this young lady's Bur-Mil Cameo "Dubbelife" hosiery, the most significant development in hosiery in years. Although very sheer, they promise to wear twice as long as other stockings... it's another reason why it pays to look for Burlington Industries triangle—a symbol of quality from the world's leading producer of hosiery, and of *all* fabrics.

"Woven into the life of America"
Burlington Quality.
This triangle means you can't buy better quality for the money.

Dior also created a slimmed down alternative look, widely copied by other designers in ready-to-wear and pattern books. This figure-hugging groomed and tailored look continued to place emphasis on the hourglass figure, and was suitable for day or evening dress, or as an elegant straight skirt and short jacket.

Known as the "sheath dress" or "wiggle dress", this sexier silhouette was preferred by movie stars such as Jane Russell and Marilyn Monroe.

Model wears Dior inspired outfit by Forstmann.
Dress patterns by Advance.

Marilyn Monroe in 1955.

Not much changed in the world of men's fashion during the 1950s. Business attire shifted just a little. Suits were slimmer, and ties were narrower. Skinny belts were worn over pleated pants. Hats, though still worn, were on the way out.

Frank Sinatra.

Marlon Brando.

James Dean.

For the younger generation however, the fashion icons of the day set the trends. James Dean and Marlon Brando made the white T-shirt and blue jeans the must-have items in casual attire. Worn alone, or under an unbuttoned shirt or jacket, the look made working class style a middle-class fashion statement.

How to avoid dry, unruly "Father Time hair"

A favorite of TV fans, our spokeswriter Bud Palmer is a fan himself . . . for new Vitalis with V-7.

New greaseless way to keep your hair neat all through 1956

Ring out the old, ring in the new! Your hair no more has need for goo. Good grooming now is very easy— For new Vitalis isn't greasy!

Vitalis keeps hair neat with V-7, the new greaseless grooming discovery. You can even use it every day for the next 366—yet never have an over-slick

plastered-down look. What's more, Vitalis protects your hair and scalp handsomely against dryness. And tests show it kills on contact the germs many doctors associate with infectious dandruff.

Give your hair a Happy New Year— try new Vitalis with V-7.

NEW VITALIS   MESSY OILS

"TISSUE TEST" PROVES GREASELESS VITALIS OUTDATES MESSY OILS. In an independent testing laboratory, Vitalis and leading cream and oil tonics were applied in the normal way. Hair was combed and then wiped with cleansing tissue. Unretouched photographs above show the difference in results!

New VITALIS® Hair Tonic with V-7

How to avoid dry, unruly "Father Time hair"

New greaseless way to keep your hair neat all through 1956

Ring out the old, ring in the new! Your hair no more has need for goo. Good grooming now is very easy–For new Vitalis isn't greasy!

Vitalis keeps hair neat with V-7, the new greaseless grooming discovery. You can even use it every day for the next 366–yet never have an over-slick plastered-down look. What's more, Vitalis protects your hair and scalp handsomely against dryness. And tests show it kills on contact the germs many doctors associate with infectious dandruff.

Give your hair a Happy New Year–try new Vitalis with V-7.

"Tissue Test" proves greaseless Vitalis outdates messy oils. In an independent testing laboratory, Vitalis and leading cream and oil tonics were applied in the normal way. Hair was combed and then wiped with cleansing tissue. Unretouched photographs above show the difference in results!

In Sports

26th Jan-5th Feb– The VII Olympic Winter Games were held in Cortina d'Ampezzo, Italy. Unusually low snowfall on the alpine slopes required snow to be trucked in from other regions by the Italian army. As no Olympic Village was built, athletes and visitors booked into local hotels or were billeted with local families.
32 countries competed in 24 events.

6th July– Wimbledon Tennis saw an all-Australian Men's Finals, as Lew Hoad beat compatriot Ken Rosewall 6-2, 4-6, 7-5, 6-4. The two Australians also joined forces to win the Men's Doubles.
Later, in September 1956, Rosewall would beat Hoad to win his first US singles title at the US National Championship Men's Tennis.

31st July– English cricketer Jim Laker set a new world record, taking 19 wickets (out of a total possible 20 wickets) during a Test Match in Manchester, England. His record stands unbeaten to this day.

22nd Nov-8th Dec– The Games of the XVI Olympiad (Summer Olympics) were held in Melbourne, Australia, the first Olympics to be held in the Southern Hemisphere. Although the "friendly games" were ultimately hailed as a great success, the months before the opening were plagued with controversy: Egypt, Iraq, Cambodia and Lebanon boycotted to protest the Suez invasion by Israel, UK and France. The Netherlands, Spain and Switzerland boycotted to protest the Soviet crushing of the Hungarian Revolution. And China boycotted to protest Taiwan's presence.

Curiously, the Equestrian event was held six months earlier in Stockholm, Sweden, as Australian quarantine rules prevented the entry of foreign horses.

Violence flared at the Hungary-USSR water polo semi-final match, as political tensions spilled into the pool. Known as the *Blood in the Water* match, Hungarian Ervin Zador was injured with a punch to the eye during the closing minutes. He required 8 stitches. Angry spectators poured onto the pool deck looking for a brawl. Hungary won 4-0, and later took the Gold Medal.

Technological Advances

June 1956– IBM released the world's first commercial Hard Disk Drive (HDD), developed as part of the accounting system for San Francisco based Zellerbach Paper.

16th September– Australia launched its first television broadcast on Channel 9 in Sydney. Broadcasts began in Melbourne two months later, just in time for telecast of the Summer Olympics.

Screen capture of Bruce Gyngell for "This is Television", TCN-9 Sydney's first television broadcast, 16th Sept 1956.

25th September– The first transatlantic telephone cable, laid between UK and Northern America, commenced operations. During the first 24 hours, 700 calls were placed from London to USA and Canada.

17th October– The world's first commercial nuclear power station was opened at Calder Hall, Cumbria, in the UK. Costing £35m to build, the plant produced electricity for 47 years. It was decommissioned in 2003.

1956– Tefal released its range of non-stick pans, a revolutionary way to make life easier for the home chef.

Other news from 1956

18th April– Actress Grace Kelly married Prince Rainier of Monaco to become Princess Grace of Monaco. The lavish reception hosted 3,000 guests, where her 142 official titles were read out. It was estimated that over 30,000 viewers watched the church ceremony, held the following day and broadcast live on TV.

24th May– The first Eurovision Song Contest was held in Lugano, Switzerland, with seven countries participating. The contest has been held annually ever since, with 2020 being the first time the competition was cancelled, due to the Covid-19 pandemic.

29th June– Actress Marilyn Monroe wed playwright Arthur Miller, in White Plains, New York, converting to Judaism for the marriage. It would be her third marriage, just one year after her divorce from baseball legend Joe DiMaggio.

30th June– Two planes collided mid-air over the Grand Canyon, Arizona, killing all 128 onboard. The United Airlines and TWA aircrafts were flying in uncontrolled airspace. It would be days before the wreckages were found. The accident was the deadliest civil aviation disaster to date, leading to the creation of the Federal Aviation Agency* in 1958.

25th July– Italian ocean liner *Andrea Doria* sank after colliding with the Swedish vessel *Stockholm* in thick fog off the coast of Nantucket in the Atlantic Ocean. Of the 1706 people on board, 51 perished, including 5 from the *Stockholm*.

* Renamed the Federal Aviation Administration in 1966.

7th August– Seven army ammunition trucks loaded with 1,053 boxes of dynamite exploded in Cali, Colombia. The trucks had been parked for the night and the cause of the explosion was never known. The blast left a crater 50m wide and 23m deep. More than 1,300 people were killed.

30th September– Three female militants of the Algerian National Liberation Front (FLN) sparked the Battle of Algiers by blowing up European targets. For the next 12 months, the FLN continued a guerilla war against the French colonialists. Algeria gained independence in 1962.

6th November– US President Dwight D. Eisenhower was re-elected for a second term, defeating Democrat candidate Adlai Stevenson.

2nd December– Fidel Castro and 81 of his fellow revolutionaries (including his brother Raoul and Argentine Marxist Che Guevara) landed in Cuba aboard the yacht Granma. Their aim, to overthrow the military junta of General Batista, was a failure, with only a small band of men surviving attacks by Batista's forces. Regrouping in the Sierra Maestra mountains, they continued enlisting new recruits, while engaging in guerilla warfare. Castro would lead his communist revolutionaries to victory in 1959.

Che Guevara & Fidel Castro in 1961.

6th December– Nelson Mandela and 155 anti-Apartheid activists were arrested in pre-dawn raids across South Africa. They were charged with high treason for their political activities. The Treason Trial dragged on for many years, with all defendants being acquitted by 1961.

1956– British author Dodie Smith wrote her best-selling book *The Hundred and One Dalmatians*. The book would inspire the 1961 Disney movie classic, two film sequels and a 1996 live action remake, in addition to a TV series and live theater productions.

Here's One Of Santa's Prize Packages

Telephones as Christmas Gifts

If you order early, we'll do our best to install your gift telephones before Christmas. If that isn't possible, then we'll come around after Christmas and install them wherever you wish.

There's a new idea in gifts and it's one of the best in a long, long time. It's the idea of giving telephones for Christmas.

Few things are so sure to be appreciated by everybody. For when you give someone an additional telephone you give three of the greatest gifts of all — comfort, convenience and security. And "it's fun to phone."

So this year, make it something different and "give the gift you'd like to get."

Save steps and work for Mother by giving her an additional telephone... for the kitchen or bedroom.

Help Dad avoid puffing up the stairs (they may be getting a little steeper, you know) by giving him a telephone in his workshop.

Reward the teen-agers who are growing up so fast with a telephone for their very own. (That could be a break for you, too!)

Easy to do. The cost is moderate. There's a choice of eight handsome colors. Ivory, beige, green, blue, red, yellow, brown and gray. Just call the Business Office of your local Bell telephone company.

BELL TELEPHONE SYSTEM

There's a new idea in gifts and it's one of the best in a long, long time. It's the idea of giving telephones for Christmas.

Few things are so sure to be appreciated by everybody. For when you give someone an additional telephone you give three of the greatest gifts of all—comfort, convenience and security. And "it's fun to phone."

So this year, make it something different and "give the gift you'd like to get."

Save steps and work for Mother by giving her an additional telephone... for the kitchen or bedroom.

Help dad avoid puffing up the stairs (they may be getting a little steeper, you know) by giving him a telephone in his workshop.

Reward the teen-agers who are growing up so fast with a telephone for their very own. (That could be a break for you, too!)

Easy to do. The cost is moderate. There's a choice of eight handsome colors. Ivory, beige, green, blue, red, yellow, brown and gray. Just call the Business Office of your local Bell telephone company.

FATHER'S DAY, JUNE 17—*He'll appreciate a box or two of his favorite cigars.*

EVER NOTICE? A MAN WHO ENJOYS CIGARS ENJOYS LIFE

His first interest is his family. Mother's problems are his problems, too. Even with those the kids bring home from school, he's there to lend a helpful hand. The secret is, he relaxes and *enjoys* life, and likes to see others enjoy it, too.

He's the kind of man who *belongs* with a cigar. It fits naturally into his way of living—because a cigar has more enjoyment, more relaxation to give.

That's why you can be so sure he'll appreciate cigars—a box or two of his favorites—for Father's Day. Remember, he needn't inhale to enjoy them—*and no pleasure so great costs so little.*

Today, every day—relax, enjoy life

HAVE A CIGAR!

Ever notice? A man who enjoys cigars enjoys life

His first interest is his family. Mother's problems are his problems, too. Even with those the kids bring home from school, he's there to lend a helpful hand. The secret is, he relaxes and *enjoys* life, and likes to see others enjoy it, too.

He's the kind of man who *belongs* with a cigar. It fits naturally into his way of living—because a cigar has more enjoyment, more relaxation to give.

That's why you can be so sure he'll appreciate cigars—a box or two of his favorites—for Father's Day. Remember, he needn't inhale to enjoy them—*and no pleasure so great costs so little.*

Today, every day—relax, enjoy life

Famous people born in 1956

1st Jan– Christine Lagarde, French lawyer & politician (Head of the IMF).

3rd Jan– Mel Gibson, Australian-American actor.

7th Jan– David Caruso, American actor.

17th Jan– Paul Young, British singer.

20th Jan– Bill Maher, American comedian & political commentator.

21st Jan– Geena Davis, American actress.

31st Jan– Johnny Rotten [John Lydon], English singer-songwriter & musician (Sex Pistols).

24th Feb– Eddie Murray, American baseballer (MLB Hall of Fame).

7th Mar– Bryan Cranston, American actor.

13th Mar– Jamie Dimon, American businessman (JPMorgan Chase CEO).

21st Mar– Ingrid Kristiansen, Norwegian long-distance world champion athlete.

17th May– Sugar Ray Leonard, American boxer.

29th May– LaToya Jackson, American singer.

6th Jun– Björn Borg, Swedish tennis player (11 Grand Slam winner).

11th Jun– Joe Montana, NFL quarterback (San Francisco 49ers).

23rd Jun– Randy Jackson, American bassist, singer, & record producer (American Idol judge).

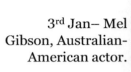

26th Jun– Chris Isaak, American singer-songwriter.

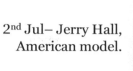
2nd Jul– Jerry Hall, American model.

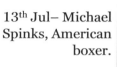
9th Jul– Tom Hanks, American actor.

13th Jul– Michael Spinks, American boxer.

25th Jul– Frances Arnold, American chemist (Nobel Prize for Chemistry 2018).

5th Aug– Maureen McCormick, American actress (Marcia-Brady Bunch).

21st Aug– Kim Cattrall, British-Canadian actress.

25th Aug– Matt Aitken, English songwriter (Stock Aitken & Waterman).

3rd Sep– Patrick McGeown, Irish IRA activist.

16th Sep– David Copperfield [Kotkin], American magician.

1st Oct– Theresa May, British Prime Minister (Conservative 2016-19).

17th Oct– Mae Jemison, 1st African American woman in space (STS 47).

18th Oct– Martina Navratilova, Czech-American tennis player.

20th Oct– Danny Boyle, English film director.

21st Oct– Carrie Fisher, American actress.

7th Dec– Larry Bird, American Basketball Hall of Fame forward, coach, executive.

7 years smooth... 90.4 proof... elegant in taste

WALKER'S DeLUXE

Best of the straight bourbons — by Hiram Walker

STRAIGHT BOURBON WHISKEY · 7 YEARS OLD · 90.4 PROOF · HIRAM WALKER & SONS INC., PEORIA, ILLINOIS

Our Walker's DeLuxe butler strikes a pleasing note for Percy Faith

Famed conductor of radio and records, Percy Faith is something of a perfectionist. That's why he liked the Walker's DeLuxe highball our butler, Robert, made him. For Walker's DeLuxe is a whiskey you can't improve on—Hiram Walker's finest bourbon. Try it soon.

7 years smooth... 90.4 proof... elegant in taste
Walker's DeLuxe
Best of the straight bourbons – by Hiram Walker

1956 in numbers

Statistics [1]

- Population of the world   2.82 billion
- Population in the United States   174.7 million
- Population in the United Kingdom   51.27 million
- Population in Canada   16.11 million
- Population in Australia   9.37 million
- Average age for marriage of women   20.1 years old
- Average age for marriage of men   22.5 years old
- USA divorce rate   23%
- Average family income USA $4,800 per year
- Minimum wage USA $1.00 per hour

Costs of Goods [2]

- Average new house $11,700
- Average new car $2,050
- New Cadillac Elderado $4,146
- A gallon of gas $0.22
- A loaf of bread $0.22
- A gallon of milk $0.97
- Smoked ham $0.27 per pound
- Coffee $0.69 per pound
- Spareribs $0.39 per pound
- Sliced Bacon $0.48 per pound
- McDonald's hamburger $0.15
- Eggs $0.79 per dozen
- Box of Kellogg's corn flakes $0.15
- Tooth paste $0.29

[1] Figures taken from worldometers.info/world-population, US National Center for Health Statistics, *Divorce and Divorce Rates* US (cdc.gov/nchs/data/series/sr_21/sr21_029.pdf) and United States Census Bureau, *Historical Marital Status Tables* (census.gov/data/tables/time-series/demo/families/marital.html).
[2] Figures from thepeoplehistory.com and mclib.info/reference/local-history-genealogy/historic-prices/1956-2/.

Image Attributions

Photographs and images used in this book are reproduced courtesy of the following:

Page 4 – Advertisement from *Readers Digest* April 1956. Source: flickr.com/photos/91591049@N00/12969367473/ by SenseiAlan. Attribution 4.0 International (CC BY 4.0).
Page 6 – Image cropped from The Travelers insurance advertisement printed in *Time* magazine 21st May 1956. Source: flickr.com/photos/91591049@N00/36770894606/. Pre 1978, no copyright mark (PD* image).
Page 7 – Source: ushistoryscene.com/article/levittown/. Pre 1978, no copyright mark (PD* image).
Page 8 – Advertisement from *Life* magazine, 5th Mar and 2nd Apr 1956. Sources: books.google.com.sg/books?id=81YEAAAA MBAJ&printsec and books.google.com.sg/books?id=OE8EAAAAMBAJ&printsec. Pre 1978, no copyright mark (PD* images).
Page 9 – Advertisement from *Time Magazine* 21st May 1956. Source: flickr.com/photos/91591049@N00/34734008505/ by SenseiAlan. Attribution 4.0 International (CC BY 4.0).
Page 10 – Leadenhall Street from Bishopsgate, 1955. Creative Commons license. Photo by Ben Brooksbank.
Page 11 – Private image, unknown creator. Pre 1978, no copyright mark (PD* image).
Page 12 – Advertisement from *Time Magazine* 4th June 1956. Pre 1978, no copyright mark (PD* image).
Page 13 – Advertisement from *Readers Digest* March 1956. Source: flickr.com/photos/91591049@N00/12305116444/ by SenseiAlan. Attribution 4.0 International (CC BY 4.0).
Page 14 – Image cropped from Champion Spark Plug advertisement printed in *Readers Digest* March 1956, source: flickr.com/photos/91591049@N00/12305118044/ by SenseiAlan. Attribution 4.0 International (CC BY 4.0).
Page 16 – MG advert from *Time Magazine* 4th June 1956. Source: flickr.com/photos/91591049@N00/32081387736/. – Austin Healey 100 advert from *Road & Track* February 1956. Source: flickr.com/photos/91591049@N00/12746288883/. – Porsche 1600 advert from *Road & Track* February 1956. Source: flickr.com/photos/91591049@N00/12792891293/. All images this page by SenseiAlan. Attribution 4.0 International (CC BY 4.0). – Chevrolet Assembly line, 1955. This image is the property of General Motors, printed here under fair use terms for information only, as it is significant to the article created. It is rendered in low resolution to avoid piracy. It is believed that this will not in any way limit the ability of the copyright owners to market or sell the product.
Page 17 – Advertisement from *Life* magazine, 2nd July 1956. Source: books.google.com.sg/books?id=7UgEAAAAMBAJ&printsec. Pre 1978, no copyright mark (PD* image).
Page 18 – Advertisement from *Life* magazine, 9th Jan 1956. Source: books.google.com.sg/books?id=ez8EAAAAMBAJ&printsec. Pre 1978, no copyright mark (PD* image).
Page 19 – 50s family, source: flickr.com/photos/95752929@N08/9018394774/. Attribution 4.0 (Creative Commons (CC) by 4.0). – *Warner Brothers Presents*, 1955-56 by Warner Brothers. Source: imdb.com/title/tt0047786/mediaviewer/ rm3026790144. This image is the property of Warner Brothers, printed here under fair use terms for information only, as it is significant to the article created. It is rendered in low resolution to avoid piracy. It is believed that this will not in any way limit the ability of the copyright owners to market or sell their product.
Page 20 – *I Love Lucy*, 1st Oct 1956, by Desilu Productions. Source: commons.wikimedia.org/wiki/File:Lucille_Ball_Orson_ Welles_I_Love_Lucy_1956.jpg. (PD image). – *General Electric Theater*, 1955 by CBS Television. Source: en.wikipedia.org/wiki/General_Electric_Theater. Pre 1978, no copyright mark (PD image).
Page 21 – *The Price is Right*, by NBC. Source: en.wikipedia.org/wiki/The_Price_Is_Right_(1956_American_game_show). (PD image). – *As the World Turns*, by CBS. Promotional photo for *The TV Guide*, 1960. Pre 1978, no copyright mark (PD image). – *The Ford Show*, source: en.wikipedia.org/wiki/The_Ford_Show (PD image). – *The Adventures of Dr. Fu Manchu*, by NBC. Source: imdb.com/title/tt0047736/mediaviewer/rm929144065. Pre 1978, (PD image).
Page 22 – Advertisement from Readers Digest October 1956. Source: flickr.com/photos/91591049@N00/14409265979/ by SenseiAlan. Attribution 4.0 International (CC BY 4.0).
Page 23 – National Highways map by Washington DC: The Association, 1958. The Library of Congress Geography and Map Division, digital ID: hdl.loc.gov/loc.gmd/g3701p.ct003465. PD image. – Missouri construction image courtesy of the US Dept of Transportation, Federal Highway Admin. Source: fhwa.dot.gov/publications/publicroads/96summer/p96su18.cfm.
Page 24 – Parliament print advertisement. Source: Ebay. Pre 1978, no mark (PD image).
Page 25 – Rosa Parks with Dr. King printed in *Ebony* Magazine, 1955. Source: en.wikipedia.org/wiki/Rosa_Parks from United States Information Agency (Bureau of Public Affairs). Pre 1978, no copyright mark (PD image). – Parks riding a bus, 21st Dec 1965, source: loc.gov/pictures/item/94505572/ from the Library of Congress, (PD image). – Parks fingerprinted by Lieutenant D.H. Lackey, 22nd Feb 1956 (PD image). – Bus 2857, source: en.wikipedia.org/wiki/Rosa_Parks. CC BY-SA 3.0. – Parks statue in the National Civil Rights Museum, Memphis, TN. Source: commons.wikimedia.org/wiki/File:Rosa_parks_ human_rights_museum_memphis_2.jpg. CC Attribution-Share Alike 4.0 International. – Parks statue at US Capitol by Eugene Daub, 2013. Source: aoc.gov/explore-capitol-campus/art/rosa-parks. (PD image).
Page 26 – Houses of Parliament, Source: commons.wikimedia.org/wiki/File:Houses_of_Parliament_and_Big_Ben.png. Licenced by the creator under Creative Commons Attribution-Share Alike 3.0 Unported. – Big Ben photo taken during the Great Smog, creator unknown. Pre 1978, no mark (PD image).
Page 27 – Sources: insider.com/vintage-photos-los-angeles-smog-pollution-epa-2020-1. – commons.wikimedia.org/ wiki/File:Two_California_Plaza_-_350_S._Grand_Avenue,_Los_Angeles.jpg. – commons.wikimedia.org/wiki/File: EAST _RIVER_AND_MANHATTAN_SKYLINE_IN_HEAVY_SMOG_-_NARA_-_548365.jpg. All images pre 1978 (PD images).
Page 28 – Airline poster images from 1956. Copyright for poster art is most likely owned by either the publisher or the creator of the work. These posters are for information only and are reproduced under fair use terms. The images are rendered in low resolution to avoid piracy. It is believed these images will not in any way limit the ability of the copyright owner to sell their product. Pre 1978, no copyright mark (PD* image).
Page 29 – Advertisement from *Time Magazine* 7th May 1956. Source: flickr.com/photos/91591049@N00/22887652764/ by SenseiAlan. Attribution 4.0 International (CC BY 4.0).
Page 30 – Missile launch, this image is the work of the U.S. federal government. Pre 1978, no mark (PD image).
Page 31 – Images: en.wikipedia.org/wiki/Hungarian_Revolution_of_1956#Social_unrest_builds. Attribution: FOTO:FORTEPAN / Pesti Srác2 & Nagy Gyula, licensed under Creative Commons Attribution-Share Alike 3.0 Unported.
Page 32 – IDF source: flickr.com/photos/idfonline/6286193672/. IDF photo archives. Creative Commons -Share Alike 3.0
Page 33 – Oil tank fire, source: commons.wikimedia.org/wiki/File:Port_Said_from_air.jpg. Photo ID: MH 23509, from the collections of the Imperial War Museums. This work created by the UK Government is in the public domain. – Ever Given, source: en.wikipedia.org/wiki/2021_Suez_Canal_obstruction. Attribution 4.0 International (CC BY 4.0).
Page 34 – Advertisement from Readers Digest December 1956. Source: flickr.com/photos/91591049@N00/12927623973/ by SenseiAlan. Attribution 4.0 International (CC BY 4.0).
Page 35 – Advertisement from *Life* magazine, 6th Feb 1956. Source: books.google.com.sg/books?id=gz8EAAAAMBAJ& printsec. Pre 1978, no copyright mark (PD* image).
Page 36 – Novak and Stewart, 1958. Source: commons.wikimedia.org/wiki/File:Kim_Novak_James_Stewart_Vertigo_ Still.jpg by Paramount Pictures. Pre 1978, no copyright mark (PD image). – Still image from video of The Redbook Awards, 1953. Image is for information only, reproduced under fair use terms in low-resolution. It is believed that this image will not devalue the ability of the copyright holders to profit from the original works. – Elvis 1956 performance, source: loc.gov/item/96500330/ from the Library of Congress, (PD image).
Page 37 – *The King and I* movie poster, 1956, by 20th Century Fox. Source: filmaffinity.com/en/film649285.html. – *Giant* movie poster, 1956, by Warner Bros. Source: en.wikipedia.org/wiki/Giant_(1956_film)#/media/File:Giant_(1956)_ poster.jpg. Copyright not renewed (PD image). – *High Society* movie poster, 1956, by MGM. Film posters, where not in the Public Domain, remain the property of the original creator. These are low-resolution images for information only, reproduced under fair use terms. It is believed that these images will not devalue the ability of the copyright holders to profit from the original works.
Page 38 – Charlton Heston in *The Ten Commandments*, 1956 by Paramount, source: en.wikipedia.org/wiki/The_Ten_ Commandments_(1956_film). Pre 1978, no copyright notice (PD image). – Audrey Hepburn and Mel Ferrer on the set of *War and Peace* in 1955, by Milton H. Greene for *LOOK Magazine* - Library of Congress, LOOK Magazine Collection. Source: en.wikipedia.org/wiki/War_and_Peace_(1956_film). All rights released per Instrument of Gift (PD image). – *War and Peace* publicity photo (Paramount, 1956). Source: classicmoviefavorites.com/henry-fonda-war-and-peace/. Pre 1978, no copyright notice (PD image).

Page 39 – *Around the World in 80 Days* movie poster, 1956, by United Artists. Source: en.wikipedia.org/wiki/ Around_the_World_in_80_Days_(1956_film). – Film Crew with elephants, creator unknown, 1956. Source: thedailystar.net/in-focus/news/when-hollywood-came-calling-1656130 – Newton, Niven, Moreno, and Cantinflas, 1956. Source: cappelleriamelegari.com/images/le-tour-du-monde-en-80-jour.jpg. Copyright for movie posters are possibly owned by either the publisher or the creator of the work depicted. Images included this page are for information only under U.S. fair use laws. The images are low resolution copies too small to be used to make illegal copies for another book. These images will not limit the copyright owner's rights to sell the products in any way.
Page 40 – Advertisement from *Time Magazine*, 4th June 1956. Source: flickr.com/photos/91591049@N00/30827487330/ by SenseiAlan. Attribution 4.0 International (CC BY 4.0).
Page 41 – Advertisement from *Time Magazine*, 21st May 1956. Source: flickr.com/photos/91591049@N00/35588514444/ by SenseiAlan. Attribution 4.0 International (CC BY 4.0).
Page 42 & 43 – Broadway: commons.wikimedia.org/wiki/Category:My_Fair_Lady_(Broadway) (PD images). – Hepburn: commons.wikimedia.org/wiki/Category:Audrey_Hepburn_in_1964#/media/File:Audrey_Hepburn_-_1964.jpg. (PD image).
Page 44 – Advertisement from *Readers Digest* April 1956. Source: flickr.com/photos/91591049@N00/14676493882/ by SenseiAlan. Attribution 4.0 International (CC BY 4.0).
Page 45 – Lewis, source: en.wikipedia.org/wiki/Jerry_Lee_Lewis. Pre 1978, no copyright mark (PD image). – Sun Records, source: commons.wikimedia.org/wiki/File:Sun_Studio,_Memphis.jpg. Pre 1978, no copyright mark (PD image). –The Million Dollar Quartet, 4th Dec 1956, Sun Records. Source: en.wikipedia.org/wiki/Million_Dollar_Quartet#/media/File: Million_Dollar_Quartet.jpg. This image is most likely owned by the person or agency who created it. It is reproduced here under Fair Use terms, as the image is not replaceable by free content. The image used is a scaled-down, low-resolution image to avoid piracy. It is believed that the use will not limit the ability of the copyright owner to sell their product.
Page 46 – The Platters publicity photo 1955. Source: en.wikipedia.org/wiki/The_Platters. Permissions CC BY-SA 3.0.
– Gogi Grant in *Dan Raven*, 1960. Source: commons.wikimedia.org/wiki/Category:Gogi_Grant. Pre 1978, (PD image).
– Doris Day publicity photo, 5th Nov 1957. Source: en.wikipedia.org/wiki/Doris_Day. Pre 1978 (PD image).
– Dean Martin publicity photo, circa 1960. Source: en.wikipedia.org/wiki/Dean_Martin. Pre 1978 (PD image).
Page 47 – Boone, circa 1960. Source: en.wikipedia.org/wiki/Pat_Boone. Pre 1978, no copyright mark (PD image). – Perry Como by NBC Television, 1956. Source: commons.wikimedia.org/wiki/File:Perry_Como_1956.JPG. PD-PRE1978 (PD image).
Page 48 – Advertisement from *Life* Magazine, 7th May 1956. Source: books.google.com.sg/books?id=V08EAAAAMBAJ& printsec. Pre 1978, no copyright mark (PD* image).
Page 49 – Advertisement from *Life* Magazine, 2nd Apr 1956. Source: books.google.com.sg/books?id=OE8EAAAAMBAJ& printsec. Pre 1978, no copyright mark (PD* image).
Page 50 – Elvis Presley, date unknown. Source: commons.wikimedia.org/wiki/Category:Elvis_Presley_in_1957. Attribution-Share Alike 4.0 International License. – Elvis Presley live, 1st Sept 1956. Source: commons.wikimedia.org/wiki/File:Elvis_ Presley_-_TV_Radio_Mirror,_September_1956_01.jpg. Pre 1978, no copyright (PD image).
Page 51 – Elvis performing in Mississippi. Source: en.wikipedia.org/wiki/File:Elvis_Presley_-_TV_Radio_Mirror,_March_ 1957_01.jpg. Uncredited photo. Pre 1978, no copyright mark (PD image). – Film poster for Love Me Tender (Paramount 1956). Source: en.wikipedia.org/wiki/Love_Me_Tender_(film). Copyright for movie posters are possibly owned by either the publisher or the creator of the work depicted. This image is for information only under U.S. fair use laws. It is low resolution copy, too small to be used to make illegal copies for another book. This image will not limit the copyright owner's rights to sell the product in any way.
Page 52 – Dresses from the *Aldens Home Order Catalog*, Summer 1956. Source: flickr.com/photos/vintage13/3682795115. Pre 1978, no copyright mark (PD image).
Page 53 – Images from myvintagevogue.com. Pre 1978, no copyright mark (PD image).
Page 54 – Dior's New Look, sketches by author. – Models wear Christian Dior, 1955. Creators unknown. Pre 1978, no copyright mark (PD image).
Page 55 – Bullet Bra advertisement from *Life* Magazine, 4th June 1956.
Source: books.google.com.sg/books?id=oEgEAAAAMBAJ&printsec. Pre 1978, no copyright mark (PD* image).
– Advertisement for Toni Todd dresses, source: *Charm Magazine*, January 1955. Pre 1978, no copyright mark (PD* image).
Page 56 – Advertisement from *Life* Magazine, 7th Nov 1956. Source: books.google.com.sg/books?id=xFQEAAAAMBAJ& printsec. Pre 1978, no copyright mark (PD* image).
Page 57 – Cover of the Lana Lobell Spring Summer Home Shopping Catalog 1956. Pre 1978, no copyright mark (PD image).
Page 58 – Advertisement from *Life* Magazine, 5th March 1956.
Source: books.google.com.sg/books?id=81YEAAAAMBAJ&printsec. Pre 1978, no copyright mark (PD* image).
Page 59 – Advertisement from *Life* Magazine, 28th Mar 1955. Source: books.google.com.sg/books?id=FIQEAAAAMBAJ& printsec. Pre 1978, no copyright mark (PD* image). – Dress patterns, source: sovintagepatterns.com/ VINTAGE-PATTERNS-1950s_c_13-6-4.html. Pre 1978, no copyright mark (PD image). – Monroe, source: commons.wikimedia.org/wiki/File: Marilyn_Monroe_at_Ciro%27s.jpg. Pre 1978, no copyright mark (PD image).
Page 60 – Sinatra, source: morrisonhotelgallery.com/collections/wtvp8g/The-Sinatra-Experience-.
– Brando, source: dailybreak.co/wp-content/uploads/2019/06/Marlon-Brando-Ford-Thunderbird-1955-Est.-2444.jpg.
– Dean, source: en.wikipedia.org/wiki/James_Dean. All images this page pre 1978, no copyright mark (PD image).
Page 61 – Advertisement from *Life* Magazine, 9th Jan 1956. Source:
books.google.com.sg/books?id=ez8EAAAAMBAJ&printsec. Pre 1978, no copyright mark (PD* image).
Page 62 – 1956 Winter Olympics Opening Ceremony. Creator unknown. Source: en.wikipedia.org/wiki/File:1956_Winter_ Olympics_opening_ceremonies.jpg. Pre 1978, no mark (PD image). – Ervin Zador, image cropped from original by AP and reproduced under U.S. fair use laws. It is a low-resolution copy, too small to be used to make illegal copies for use in another book. It is believed the use of this image will not limit the copyright owner's rights to sell the product in any way.
Page 63 – Screen capture from "This is Television" by TCN-9 Sydney. The copyright for this image is most likely owned by the company or corporation that produced it. The image is reproduced here for information only under Australian and U.S. fair use laws. It is a low-resolution copy, too small to be used to make illegal copies for use in another book. It is believed the use of this image will not limit the copyright owner's rights to sell the product in any way.
Source: en.wikipedia.org/wiki/File:WelcomeToTelevision.jpg – Calder Hall nuclear power station. Source: en.wikipedia.org/wiki/Nuclear_power#/media/ File:Calder_Hall_nuclear_power_station_(11823864155).jpg (PD image).
Page 64 – Grace Kelly from *MGM Parade*, produced by MGM and aired on her wedding day. Source: commons.wikimedia.org/wiki/File:Grace_Kelly.JPG under Creative Commons Attribution-Share Alike 3.0 – Marilyn Monroe and Arthur Miller at their wedding from *TV-Radio Mirror*, May 1961. Source: commons.wikimedia.org/wiki/Category: Marilyn_Monroe_in_1956#/media/File:Monroe_Miller_Wedding.jpg (PD image). – Andrea Doria by US Coast Guard Service. Source: en.wikipedia.org/wiki/File:Andrea_Doria_USCG_1.jpg. A work of the U.S. federal government (PD image).
Page 65 – Guevara & Castro by Alberto Korda. Source: Museo Che Guevara, Havana Cuba. Pre 1978, no copyright mark (PD image). – First edition book cover, 1956, by Dodie Smith. The copyright is most likely owned by the creator and is reproduced here under US fair use laws. It is a low-resolution copy, too small to be used to make illegal copies for use in another book. It is believed the use of this image will not limit the copyright owner's rights to sell the product in any way.
Page 66 – Advertisement from *Readers Digest*, December 1956. Source: flickr.com/photos/91591049@N00/15737287867/ by SenseiAlan. Attribution 4.0 International (CC BY 4.0).
Page 67 – Advertisement from *Life* magazine, 4th June 1956. Source: books.google.com.sg/books?id=oEgEAAAAMBAJ& printsec. Pre 1978, no copyright mark (PD* image).
Page 68 & 69 – All photos are, where possible, CC BY 2.0 or PD images made available by the creator for free use including commercial use. Where commercial use photos are unavailable, photos are included here for information only under U.S. fair use laws due to: 1- images are low resolution copies; 2- images do not devalue the ability of the copyright holders to profit from the original works in any way; 3- Images are too small to be used to make illegal copies for use in another book; 4- The images are relevant to the article created.
Page 70 – Advertisement from *Life* magazine, 4th June 1956. Source: books.google.com.sg/books?id=oEgEAAAAMBAJ& printsec. Pre 1978, no copyright mark (PD* image).

*Advertisements (or images from advertisements) published in a collective work (such as a magazine or periodical issue) in the United States between 1925 and 1977, and without a valid and current copyright notice specific to the advertisements, have fallen into the public domain under current USA copyright laws.

These words first appeared in print in the year 1956.

antimissile · PSYCHEDELIC · margarita · all-terrain vehicle · wash-and-wear · polycystic ovary syndrome · gobsmacked · Quantum leap · glitz · rockabilly · snooze button · MERITOCRACY · felt-tip · microcomputer · KITTEN HEEL · GREEN CARD · Meltdown

*From merriam-webster.com/time-traveler/1956.

Please help me out:

I sincerely hope you enjoyed reading this book and that it brought back many fond memories from the past.

I have enjoyed researching and writing this book for you and would greatly appreciate your feedback by way of a written review and/or star rating.

First and foremost, I am always looking to grow and improve as a writer. It is reassuring to hear what works, as well as to receive constructive feedback on what could improve.

Second, starting out as an unknown author is exceedingly difficult, and Customer Reviews go a long way toward making the journey out of anonymity possible.

Please help me by taking a few moments to leave a review for others to read.

Best regards,
Bernard Bradforsand-Tyler.

Please leave a
book review/rating at:

http://bit.ly/1956reviews

Or scan the QR code:

Printed in Great Britain
by Amazon

67049526R00043